REDEFINING ANXIETY

What It Is, What It's Not, and How to Get Your Life Back

Dr. John Delony

RAMSEY
P R E S S

Published by Ramsey Press, The Lampo Group, LLC
Franklin, Tennessee 37064

This publication is designed to provide accurate and authoritative information with regard to the subject matter covered. It is sold with the understanding that the publisher is not engaged in rendering mental health or other professional advice. If expert assistance is required, the services of a competent professional should be sought.

Unless otherwise noted, Scripture quotations are from the NEW AMERICAN STANDARD BIBLE®, Copyright © 1960, 1962, 1963, 1968, 1971, 1972, 1973, 1975, 1977, 1995 by The Lockman Foundation. Used by permission.

Editorial: Rachel Knapp and Jennifer Day
Cover Design: Chris Carrico
Interior Design: Mandi Cofer

ISBN: 978-1-9421-2144-2

Printed in the United States of America
22 23 24 25 26 POL 10 9 8 7 6

Anxiety in a man's heart weighs it down,

but a good word makes it glad.

—PROVERBS 12:25

INTRODUCTION

My eyes shot open at 2:35 a.m. Again.

I sat straight up in bed, heart racing, bitten with anger and frustration.

I woke up almost every night between the witching hours of 2:00 a.m. and 3:30 a.m. It was maddening. It didn't matter whether I took prescription sleep medicine, made a lavender-infused essential oil potion, did deep breathing and yoga, or tried any number of the faux pop-psychological offerings the internet had to offer. Without fail, I would collapse from exhaustion sometime after 10:00 p.m. and be wide awake a few short hours later.

I remember getting to a point where going to sleep was so frustrating that I would get anxious thinking about waking up anxious.

This was not a life.

On this particular Texas morning, my body ripped me from sleep, letting me know it sensed danger and disconnection. Of course, there was no immediate danger. I was healthy, my wife was asleep next to me, my beautiful child was asleep in the next room, and my stable job was not going anywhere.

But my body sensed danger. It always sensed danger. Or disconnection. Or a lack of control.

This set my heart racing and my stomach flooded with a familiar warmth—a confusing and damning mix of brain chemicals that caused me to either fight, flight, or freeze. The regulators inside my mind and body no longer cared for nuance or truth. Feelings ruled—and on the inside, everything was spinning a hundred miles an hour.

Sadly, this wasn't just affecting me. I knew my anxiety was burning up my work relationships, my marriage, my relationships with my new son and my friends. I was electric. I kept thinking bad or stressful things were coming, and I was frustrated that no one around me saw the dragons.

And make no mistake: I was doing a hero's job holding things together. On the outside, I was doing great.

I had three degrees, including a PhD. Professionally, I worked at a university where I managed multiple departments, hundreds of staff and paraprofessional employees, and millions of revenue and expense dollars across a dozen or so accounts. I was on call 24/7 and made hospital visits in the middle of the night a few times a week. I responded to students' mental health breakdowns, and hugged parents through tragedies. I was responsible for crisis response across the thousands of students living on campus, taught graduate courses, and had an amazing family. I was a leader at a faith-based university, in the midst of my own deep faith crisis, a fledgling member of a local church, and I was desperately trying to emerge from a cocoon of old beliefs, privilege, and bad theology.

I wasn't stupid. I wasn't irresponsible. I loved everyone and I always showed up. I was living the dream.

But I couldn't shake this feeling that I was malfunctioning. That I was breaking apart in my own skin.

After lying in bed for hours that morning, waiting for the sun to come up and burn off my catastrophic thoughts and my intrusive memories, I got out of bed, got dressed, and headed to work.

I began to walk across campus to my office . . . when I just stopped. I couldn't take another step forward. I paused for several moments in the Texas sun, spun around, walked to the parking lot, and hopped into my wife's little Corolla.

Without a word to my team or my wife, I left campus and drove several hours away—to a completely different city— where I had a close friend who also happened to be a brilliant medical doctor. I arrived at his office and burst past his receptionist, past his lab testing area, and crashed into his office.

He looked up from his desk and said, "Delony? What are you doing here?"

He was as surprised to find me standing in his office as I was.

I took a deep breath and looked him in the eye and said, "Dude . . . something is wrong with me. I'm losing my mind. And I need help."

You Mean I'm Not All Alone?

Soon after that day in my friend's office, I began a long, windy road to figure out what happened. I had to know what was wrong with my brain.

I went to therapy. I took medication. My wife and I took a huge pay cut so I could take a new job. I learned some things at Harvard and spent a year with a professor who helped me practice meditation. I got a second PhD, this time in counseling. I worked with SWAT and police teams as a crisis responder, counseled clients, and traveled across the country speaking to other counselors, academics, and everyday folks like you and me. I spent time reimagining friendships and reconnecting with loved ones. I sought out mentors and submitted to their wisdom and insight. My family suffered multiple tragic losses, we had a second child, and I almost imploded my marriage a few times—but we hung on and tilled the soil deeply and forever.

And I discovered something that changed my life: anxiety is not the problem.

Anxiety is just a symptom.

Anxiety is a signal.

I'll say it again: *anxiety is not the problem.*

> " Currently in the United States, anxiety affects more than forty million adults—and that number is only increasing and often highly under-reported. "

If you were to read the statistics, you would think that anxiety had suddenly descended upon the human race, like a dark, heavy plague. Currently in the United States, anxiety affects more than forty million adults—and that number is only increasing and often highly under-reported.[1]

We're being told there is something broken inside of us. That *we're* broken and only a professional can fix us. We are a diagnosis, an insurance code, a label. But that's not the whole story.

What Is Anxiety?

Now before you get indignant and say mean things about me on the interwebs, and before you call the League of Diagnosis Defenders (not a real thing), hear me out.

The terms *anxiety* and *anxiety disorder* are often used interchangeably. Medical and mental health professionals refer to what's called a "clinical diagnostic manual" to formally define and diagnose someone with an anxiety disorder. The most common manual in the United States is the *Diagnostic and Statistical Manual of Mental Disorders* (DSM). With few exceptions, I'm not a fan of the DSM or most mental health diagnoses in general. In almost every situation, I despise the DSM as much as my friend Dave Ramsey despises the FICO score.

Formally, the DSM defines an anxiety disorder like this:

Excessive anxiety and worry (apprehensive expectation), occurring more days than not for at least six months, about a number of events or activities (such as work or school performance). [Additionally], the anxiety and worry are associated with three or more of the following six symptoms (with at least some symptoms present for more days than not for the past six months): restlessness, feeling keyed up or on edge; being easily fatigued; difficulty concentrating or mind going blank; irritability; muscle tension; sleep disturbance (difficulty falling or staying asleep, or restless, unsatisfying sleep); and intrusive (unwelcome and disturbing) thoughts.[2]

While this definition can be helpful in certain situations, for most of us, it's incomplete—and it's definitely not helpful.

Here's the full story: *Anxiety is just an alarm system.* Nothing more and nothing less. Anxiety is our body's internal notification that our brain is detecting danger,

that our body is in desperate need of sleep and restoration,

that we are disconnected from our tribe or community,

or that we are lonely.

Our anxiety alarms cause restlessness, racing hearts, panic attacks, a stomach drop, hypervigilance, and looping, intrusive thoughts. They do this because it's our body's way of screaming, "DANGER! NOT SAFE! RUN!"

But . . .

Anxiety is not a permanent medical condition. Anxiety is not an identity. Anxiety shouldn't be a way of being, an excuse, or a reason for giving up on connection and joy.

> ## " Anxiety is not a permanent medical condition. "

It's just an alarm. And in our never-ending quest to avoid pain, negative consequences, or uncomfortable feelings of any kind, we've channeled all of our spiritual, pharmaceutical, medical, and psychological energies into trying to fix or disable the alarm system instead of putting out the fires and clearing out the smoke.

Friends, the alarm is not the problem.

The problem is the psychotic and destructive ecosystem that we call "normal life," filled with busyness, disconnection, clichés, influencers, and *more* of everything. On top of it all, some of us have been born into raging fires of poverty, racism, or abuse. And now we're annoyed that our hearts and minds are sounding the sirens.

The alarm is not the problem.

The alarm is just trying to save our lives.

So, What Do We Do Now?

What does this mean for the millions of us who struggle with anxiety symptoms? What does it mean for the countless people bending low under the weight of our own bodies betraying us— who know we are safe but our heart rates, intrusive thoughts, impulsive behaviors, and exhausted bodies are no longer serving us well? What about the millions of other people who have been robotically churning along, living lives of avoidance, solitude, addiction, or fantasy—all of which are ways we try to duct-tape a pillow over the alarm without having to address the fire and the smoke in the room? Worse, what about the millions of people who are stuck in debilitating negative thought spirals, in abusive relationships, in oppressive systems, or other nightmarish economic, sociological, or psychological cages? Or more recently, what do you do when the alarms are ringing due to an unforeseen pandemic, real job loss, or fear and uncertainty about the future?

Please hear me on this singularly important point:

There is light at the end of the tunnel.

You can get your life back. And it starts today with this Quick Read. We're going to talk through four of the biggest myths we've been told about anxiety—and what's really true. Then we're going to look at what you can start doing immediately, and for the long haul, so you can begin to experience less stress and worry and start moving forward with your life.

PART 1: THE MYTHS WE BELIEVE ABOUT ANXIETY

Throughout my career working at multiple universities, I witnessed a lot of move-in days, with nervous parents and wide-eyed freshmen unpacking belongings and settling into their new homes. I remember one mom, Sarah, who broke down while saying goodbye to her daughter. Sarah started breathing hard, crying uncontrollably, and eventually launched into a full-blown panic attack. Her body was trying to get her attention. She came into my office and sat down on the couch. She couldn't breathe, she felt like the walls were closing in, and her heart was racing.

As her breathing slowed and she regained her composure, she opened up to me about the racing thoughts carving up her mind: *Did I do enough to prepare my little girl for the real world? What if my daughter hangs with the wrong crowd? What am I going to do when I go back home and walk by her empty bedroom? I'm going to have to face the marriage I've been avoiding for so long . . .* When Sarah started to share her thoughts with me, I could have explained it away with the sayings we've all heard before: *You're going to be fine. I'm sure your husband loves you. You just need some "you" time. You must have some sort of genetic tendency toward anxiety. Just relax. Get a hold of yourself.* But one-liners like these aren't helpful—in fact, they can be damaging.

> **Anxiety alarms are real. When your thoughts spin out of control and your body begins to betray you, it's terrifying.**

Anxiety alarms are real. When your thoughts spin out of control and your body begins to betray you, it's terrifying. I sat with Sarah and helped her acknowledge and normalize the alarms that were sounding in her heart and mind. And because she was a brilliant, loving mom, she was eventually able to put her finger on the root problem: facing an empty nest, a struggling marriage, and sorrow because her little girl was leaving home. Sarah's marriage had been slipping away for years and her daughter had given her someone to love and hold on to. Sarah had not worked in years and now that her last child was out of the house, she was facing the hard task of figuring out what she would do next. Sarah's life was on relational life support and transforming into something completely new. Her body was letting her know that it was overwhelmed. Her alarms were letting her know that danger, a lack of control, and loneliness were upon her!

Sarah didn't need me to give her a pep talk and some clever advice and send her on her way. She needed me to be present, acknowledge her physical symptoms, trust and honor her feelings, and let her regain control over her intrusive thoughts. I recommended that she meet with a counselor who could begin to walk with her during her upcoming life transitions. I let her know that she was not broken or crazy. This type of response flies in the face of our culture, which is more likely to offer up cute (and lame) advice ripped off of Instagram, Pinterest boards, or CrossFit gym chalkboards. Most of the time, this advice isn't helpful or even true.

When it comes to anxiety, myths are everywhere! I'm sure you've heard, or even said, some of them before. Myths about anxiety include:

Anxiety is a disease.

Anxiety is caused by your genetics, and you inherit this destiny from your parents or grandparents.

If you have anxiety, you are broken and there is something wrong with you.

Anxiety only affects lazy, weak, or undisciplined people.

If you're anxious, you're probably hiding something from your loved ones, from God, or yourself.

What is the matter with you? Chill out . . . and quit acting all nervous and fidgety and worried.

Anxiety is just stress. We all worry. Get over it.

People with anxiety probably just want attention.

Anxiety can be fixed with yoga, breathing, and a better attitude.

Anxiety can only be cured through medicine.

Everyone has an opinion about anxiety or a personal experience with anxiety. Everyone has a brother in college or a friend or a professor or a church pastor who considers themselves an expert in anxiety, panic, worry, or stress. A simple google search of the word *anxiety* offers more than 331 million results. Wow. The fact and fiction of anxiety are often woven together, presenting a confusing, and sometimes deceptive, picture of reality. While I believe that most people (other than drug companies) are trying to help, the things we've heard about anxiety are generally partial truths at best and complete myths at worst. Let's dive in and start to untangle what isn't true about anxiety.

Myth #1: Anxiety is a disease or genetic condition.

You've likely heard—even from mental health and medical professionals—that anxiety is a medical and/or genetic condition. You may have even heard or read the research headlines suggesting that generational trauma and stress responses are passed down from generation to generation. These headlines seem to suggest that if you have certain genes, you are predestined to suffer from anxiety—and there's nothing you can do about it. Such is your lot in life. Fortunately, this is not an accurate telling of the story.

> **Is a person with a certain genetic tendency toward anxiety destined to live a life of anxiety and chaos? Absolutely not.**

Follow me on a quick elementary science class refresher. Hopefully, you remember that you inherit traits like hair color, eye color, height, and bone structure from your parents. You also inherit all sorts of personality, physical, and environmental tendencies from your parents. For instance, based on the genetic cocktail I received from my parents and the environment I was raised in, my brain might release more or less stress hormones and brain chemicals than yours during a scary movie or an uncomfortable conversation. My genetic/environmental cocktail might make my heart race a bit faster and my shoulders tense up more than yours. That's because everyone is born with a unique combination of traits and into different home environments (even siblings raised by the same parents will experience their environment differently).

But is a person with a certain genetic tendency toward anxiety destined to live a life of anxiety and chaos? Absolutely not. As Brené Brown clarifies, "Genetics loads the gun and the environment pulls the trigger."[3]

So what does this mean? It means that genetics is only a role player—not a main actor—in the story of our lives. Our experiences and environments are the stars of the show. Point blank: genetics can make you more inclined toward anxiety, but it does not have the final word on how you live your life—not even close. This is good news! Thankfully, you have a role to play in the choose-your-own-adventure story of your life. You don't have to let surviving an abusive childhood, a traumatic event, a jerk boss in a thankless job, or three kids and a passive-aggressive spouse sentence you to a lifetime of ringing anxiety alarms. There is healing on the other side of anxiety.

You Are Not a Machine to Be Fixed

The relationship among anxiety, genetics, and environment is complex. And when it comes to our health, wholeness, and joy, we don't like complex. Here in the United States, most people hold a simplistic view of health. We've reduced the complexity and interactions of the human body, heart, and mind to a series of parts, much like a machine. Think Legos or vehicle parts. We often treat visits to the doctor like taking our car into the shop. We explain to the doctor the noises or smells we are making, and we get our diagnostic tests. If something is wrong with us, there must be something off in the "machine": the wiring, the parts, or the fuel. Unfortunately, research scientists, specialized medical doctors, and medical schools have created artificial boundaries for distinct parts of the body so they can study them as individual pieces. Over time, this has caused us to view ourselves in parts and not as a whole person.

Why am I telling you this? We must stop separating parts of our health and well-being. Most of the time, there is little to no difference between heart health, gut health, mental health, and skin health. You are all of these things, all at the same time. A person might struggle to lose weight due to stress, food intake, a hurt foot, depression, lack of exercise, or drinking too much. A person with excessive stress and anxiety might end up with skin issues, weight gain, heart disease, joint pain, back pain, and so forth. Your mental and physical health are one and the same and must be addressed as a whole.

It's important to point out that anxiety alarms *are* biological phenomenon happening in your body. Cells fire, chemicals flow, hearts push blood, and lungs process the inflow and outflow of air. Skin tingles, nerves burn, and pupils narrow. Trillions of biological interactions take place every day. But the over-simplified medical obsession with biological origins and solutions has proven dangerously overblown. For all of the hype surrounding biology, there are no blood tests or MRIs to even prove an anxiety diagnosis.[4]

And yet, anxiety has been lumped into the same category as cancer or type 1 diabetes. The assumption is that anxiety is just something you can get, like a cold, or something that you inherit from generations before you. We are led to believe that anxiety is a disease, a malfunction, or a broken part of our brain or body. Once you get (or inherit) anxiety, you are stuck managing it forever. This is a dangerous and frustrating lie.

People are not machines to be fixed, computers to be rewired, or puzzles to be solved. People are relational beings to be with.

We are vastly complex organisms, made up of living connec-
tions, thoughts, and feelings, charged with electricity and water,
and highly impacted by internal and external environments. It's
actually wild and beautiful how everything is all connected—
your mind, body, and spirit. That's why anxiety can't be reduced
to simply genetics or disease. Your relationships, work, thoughts,
environment, genetics, and actions all add up to who you are and
have a significant impact on your anxiety.

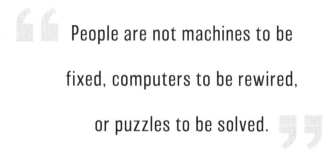

> People are not machines to be
> fixed, computers to be rewired,
> or puzzles to be solved.

Myth #2: Anxiety can only be
cured with medication.

When we reduce anxiety down to a medical disease, a foregone
genetic conclusion, or a part of a broken or malfunctioning
system, the next logical step is to ask: is there a pill for that? I
understand why trying to find a pill to solve the anxiety problem is so appealing. If anxiety is just a medical problem we can
fix with a pill, we don't have to do the hard work of looking
at and changing our lives. We don't have to examine our relationships, the disconnection between our dreams and realities,

our lack of exercise and self-care, or the systemic issues in our culture. We especially don't have to stare down past traumas and abuses. If it's all a medical issue, I can just take a pill, skip all of that pain and work, and head out into the world feeling "happy."

Let's be honest: as a society, we are *way, way* overmedicated. We have turned almost every up and down of normal life into a disease or a medical issue. Some people are really trying to use science to help, while others just want to sell more drugs and medications. We've turned every uncomfortable feeling, thought, pain, or emotion into a medical condition. I am not a medical doctor and recognize that there are plenty of unique situations that require medical interventions, so I will not belabor the point or step too far out of my lane. But understand this: despite a massive increase in the use of medications for anxiety, no country in the world is seeing a reduction in the number of diagnoses.[5] Despite the billions and billions of dollars spent on anxiety medications, the anxiety problem is only getting worse.[6]

When we reduce anxiety to a condition that can only be solved with medication, we surrender responsibility to take control of our lives and make changes to our environments and our family trees. We end up handing the problem off to our doctor and pharmaceutical companies to fix. This gives us an excuse to throw in the towel and bury our face in our hands in defeat.

Please don't give up on yourself. You are worth your full attention.

How many times have you heard someone say, "I would have done it, but I have anxiety . . . " or "My anxiety makes me . . . " or "I was late because of my anxiety . . . " or "I can't sleep / exercise / be kind / show up because of my anxiety"? The bigger gap we can wedge between biology and personal responsibility, the better we feel about outsourcing our personal health to other people. Then we can release ourselves from taking full ownership of healing broken relationships, ending abusive relationships, learning to manage our thoughts, and choosing to get well. The good and the bad news is this: only we can choose a life of wellness and healing. We have to take responsibility if we want to grow and move forward.

> " Despite the billions and billions
>
> of dollars spent on anxiety
>
> medications, the anxiety problem
>
> is only getting worse. "

If you're struggling with anxiety, remember you probably don't have a disease that can only be solved with medications. Instead, you may be stuck in or choosing an unsustainable, overwhelming life—dragged into or leaning into the chaos and disconnection of our modern world. Or you may have found yourself lonely and without relationships. But you can change.

Make no mistake: this is really, really hard. We're all addicted to comfort, and we're all addicted to quick fixes. We don't know how to have uncomfortable conversations about our needs. We feel trapped between values and felt obligations. We avoid every difficult feeling, and we've taken to playing whack-a-mole with our brain chemistry—trying everything we can to get rid of our hard choices and difficult feelings without actually confronting the hard and uncomfortable realities we are living in. This is dangerous and highly unsettling.

My Journey with Medication

About a decade ago, I allowed my anxiety alarms to get too loud and debilitating. I ran, pushed, avoided, and denied myself right into a ditch. The alarms became so loud and so overwhelming that I was unable to do anything except cover my ears and hide under the covers. So, for a season, I took a reduced amount of anxiety medication. I found medication very helpful to turn down my body's anxiety alarms so I could actually do the work of meeting with mentors, restoring my marriage, spending time with mental health professionals, changing my sleep and diet, taking a deep and honest look at my relationships, and making the necessary changes to move forward in life. If you're considering taking medication for anxiety or you're considering stopping your medication, you must work with the right medical professional before jumping in or out of the pool.

When I met with my doctors (both a traditional medical doctor and a licensed holistic doctor), I told them that I would not put a pill in my mouth before having a planned exit strategy for transitioning off of the medication. I wanted to make sure my doctors were experts, teachers, and partners in my wellness journey. I wanted them to know that I was grateful for their expertise and partnership but that I wanted to take full ownership and responsibility for my long-term health. Not surprisingly, my two doctors were extraordinary. They answered my questions and recommended supplements and dietary changes. They were not afraid for me to challenge them, and they gladly supported my desire to take ownership of my heart, mind, and spirit.

> In the short term, medication can be a wonderful way to tone down the alarms that are constantly ringing, giving you a chance to catch your breath and do the deeper work that leads to lasting change.

Medicine helped me take my hands off my ears and connect with my community, mentors, and a counselor. In the end, anxiety medication didn't fix my life, it didn't change my identity, and it didn't heal my traumas. I had to be vulnerable, humble, and work really hard.

I want to really be clear on this point: I don't believe that anxiety medications are always wrong or bad. The right medication can turn off or lower the volume of the alarms. If they're helpful for a season, take them. In the short term, medication can be a wonderful way to tone down the alarms that are constantly ringing, giving you a chance to catch your breath and do the deeper work that leads to lasting change.

But before anyone takes a pill for anxiety, I want them to enter into that relationship with open eyes and an informed mind. Each and every pill for anxiety triggers a highly complex and interactive process in your brain, so develop a partnership with your doctor and counselor.

Once again, I'm way oversimplifying here, but at the end of the day, all anxiety medications can do is dial down or temporarily turn off the alarms. Silencing the alarm doesn't fix the problem. It doesn't stop the anxiety raging in your heart, in your relationships, or in your past. In almost every situation, *medication is not a long-term solution to anxiety. You are.*

Myth #3: Anxiety is an identity or a destiny.

If you walk into a doctor's or counselor's office with the signs and symptoms of anxiety or related disorders, you might walk out with a new diagnostic label for some variation of an anxiety disorder. I mentioned this before, but I think it's important to say again: mental health experts and medical doctors diagnose anxiety, depression, and other things just like they diagnose strep, cancer, or the flu—but with way less precision. With strep, cancer, or the flu, doctors give tests for bacteria, cancer cells, or a virus to determine the presence of a pathogen. But not so with mental health challenges. Mental health diagnoses are usually based on self-reported questionnaires, professional experience, or gut feelings. A common anxiety questionnaire might ask for the severity of the anxious feelings, the length of time a person has been feeling anxious, and how disruptive the anxiety is to the daily routine. Again, there are no blood or bacteria tests for anxiety. Needless to say, in most cases, I am not a fan.

But to be fair, while I often criticize the majority of mental health diagnoses, there are times when a diagnosis might be perceived by some as helpful. A diagnosis can be a way to "name the dragon" and provide an acknowledgment and label for the pain and havoc inside yourself or a loved one. Sometimes a label allows a struggling person to identify specific resources, go to appropriate professionals, and have a healing target to work toward. These are generally all good things. But there is a dark side to many mental health diagnoses.

> Just because someone gives the dragon a name doesn't mean the dragon gets to move in and live with you.

While mental health diagnoses can help us name the dragons, they can also easily sink into our subconscious and become our identity. When we are labeled with a psychological impairment, we can come to believe that we are dysfunctional, broken, or disordered. Just because someone gives the dragon a name doesn't mean the dragon gets to move in and live with you. You don't have to keep it as a pet and tattoo its face on your arm. You don't have to let it become part of who you are.

If you come to believe that anxiety is your identity, you can easily fall into the trap of believing it's your destiny. It's easy to give into the idea that because you have been diagnosed with anxiety, you will always be anxious, just like you will always be the height that you are or have the eye color that you have. This is false. Anxiety most often comes and goes in seasons, and it doesn't have to be forever.

You Are More than Your Anxiety

Humans are storytellers. We make sense of the world through stringing events together and giving them meaning. We look everywhere in our lives for evidence that our stories are correct—and we usually find what we're looking for. When we encounter a confusing or painful situation that doesn't make sense, we fill in the gaps with stories we make up. But far too often, we insert destructive and negative narratives about who we are. It's super important to note that when our anxiety alarms are going off, we are more inclined to see angry faces and to assume the worst about someone's intentions. Our brain figures that the best way to keep us safe is to assume everyone is out to get us—that way, we have less of a chance of getting hurt. In the same way, we take on the labels, the diagnoses, and the identities we are given. When someone tells you a story—*you have anxiety*—you have a choice to live into that identity or not. It is the difference between thinking, *I have a disorder* versus *I am in a tough season.* One is an identity; the other is a temporary circumstance.

Anxiety becomes a default brain response for moments when you feel out of control, not in charge, or not safe. And if you constantly think you're not in control of your own actions and thoughts, right down to your ability to choose between Netflix or exercise and positive or negative thoughts, your brain will continually sound the anxiety alarms. If you walk around with your shoulders slumped under the weight of your anxiety diagnosis and don't express your needs, desires, or personal boundaries, the alarms will sound again. Or if you remain stuck in an unsafe or traumatic environment, bury trauma, and tell yourself that this is your lot in life and things will never change, the anxiety alarms will never stop screaming. But it doesn't have to be this way! You can choose a different way.

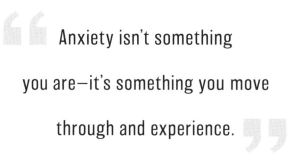

Anxiety isn't something you are—it's something you move through and experience.

Anxiety isn't something you are—it's something you move through and experience. Let's take Emma, for example. Emma went through a dark season of anxiety as she navigated the world in her midtwenties. Emma felt overworked at her crummy job at a fast-paced start-up. She was lonely and disconnected from community, and stress settled in her body to create chronic back pain and intense headaches. One weekend she broke away from work and went skiing with her family. As she was riding the lift with her sister on a snowy afternoon, Emma opened up about the crushing fear and loneliness she was experiencing. Emma's sister held her close and, after a quiet moment, said, "You can't see the mountains right now because it's snowing, right? But you saw them yesterday. And when the storm has passed, you'll see them again." In an instant, Emma was able to get perspective on her anxiety. Yes, the "blizzard" of her life was scary and overwhelming. But the anxiety alarms were trying to get her attention just *as they were designed to.*

> " You are more than your past trauma and your deepest hurt. You are more than your mistakes and your failures. "

Here's the part that excites me most: in this moment of clarity, Emma recognized that she could choose to face and head into the storm! Emma knew that when she took steps to change her life, the alarms would quiet down. So after the ski trip, she immediately started looking for a new job. She painted a picture of what she wanted her life to look like, and now she's working to make it a reality. It took a few months of searching, but eventually, Emma took a job in another state and she is now investing in her new friendships, growing at work, and experiencing tremendous freedom. And those alarms? They've quieted down. They're not trying to warn her of danger any-more. Emma's world is falling back into balance.

Rejecting anxiety as an identity means that you must take responsibility for your life, just like Emma did. You cannot control everything, and some storms will rage on for a while until they've run their course. Stressful seasons are a part of each of our lives. Wars happen, family members get sick. Loved ones die and jobs disappear. But when you decide to focus on what you *can* control, and you choose to put the other things down, you can start rebalancing your life.

Know this: You are more than your past trauma and your deepest hurt. You are more than your mistakes and your failures. Your identity does not rest in the worst thing that has ever happened to you. Yes, it's necessary to acknowledge our anxiety, our struggles, and our trauma. But ultimately, we get to decide that we want to move through them, heal from them, and work to create a joyful, relational, and extraordinary life on the other side.

Myth #4: You can have and do it all, at the same time, without major trade-offs and consequences.

"You can be anything you want to be! Just set your mind to it and you can do it!"

"If you can dream it, you can make it happen!"

"If you want it bad enough, you can accomplish anything!"

You've heard nonsense like this, right? Most of us have grown up with these well-intentioned, but harmful, lies running through our heads. We have ridiculous and unrealistic expectations of who we can—and should—become and what we can—and must—accomplish. We believe it's possible to be it all, do it all, and have it all—all at the same time and with no trade-offs. This irrational confidence in our own ability, combined with unrealistic expectations, has horrible consequences for our total health and well-being. We waste so much time planning for greener grass that we don't breathe the air of our current mornings.

> "We waste so much time planning for greener grass that we don't breathe the air of our current mornings."

When my son was seven, his teacher asked him where he was planning to go to college. She wanted him to start thinking about his college major. He was SEVEN. Teenagers are pressured to have their five-, ten-, and twenty-year plans in place, beginning with their internships and volunteer opportunities, and ending with their appointment as CEO to some imaginary company. Women are burdened by the expectations that they need to strive for that VP position at work, plan the perfect Pinterest-y birthday party, and still be an ever-present, totally engaged mother. Men are pressured to always achieve and conquer while never showing a desire for intimate relationships or letting others glimpse into the inner workings of their hearts. Recently, I got a message from a man who said that men are not human *beings*; they are human *doings*.

Seriously? Stop it.

Everything has a cost. You cannot be everything to everyone all at the same time. I bought into this lie early on. About a decade ago, my life was so chaotic and unsustainable that it reached a boiling point. Between the two of us, my wife and I had earned six degrees, and we managed to rack up six-figures worth of student debt along the way. We were living in a house we couldn't afford and just had our first kid. I was running on an uphill treadmill of work: on call 24/7/365 while working two extra jobs and always gunning for the next promotion. I applied for dozens of jobs while always searching for something else. I was white-knuckling my way through life, refusing to let anything go, but always looking to jump ship. Unsurprisingly, my alarms rang constantly.

Trying to do it all—keeping up with the grind at work, hitting the gym five times a week, attending every game and dance recital, being a homeroom parent, keeping the house spotless, hosting book clubs and happy hours, thumbs-upping all of your friends' posts, being the best friend who remembers every single birthday, handling the pandemic with grace and dignity, keeping perfect hair, and not flipping off the idiot who cut you off in traffic—it's exhausting. It's fantasy. It's not possible. I don't care how much you've dreamed it or spoken it into being.

We all feel burdened by having too much on our plates all the time. And to make matters worse, we can feel like shameful, incomplete losers as soon as we pull out our phones and scroll through our social media feeds. We compare curated, fantasy pictures of babies, vacations, birthday parties, and workouts with our real-life zits, cellulite, rained-out fishing trips, and poor lighting. Industries exist to keep us feeling empty, less-than, and anxious. They have hacked our attention and our feelings to keep us constantly glued to our devices.

So, we have tied our self-worth to impossible, ever-moving standards. Chasing these standards makes us feel out of step and isolated—which in turn, sounds the alarms of disconnection and danger. Hear me when I say this:

there is no finish line,

no carefree life,

it's all a lie.

You simply can't do and have it all.

The hard, but freeing, truth about life is that we can—and must—make choices. We need to do the hard work of deciding what we actually want and what trades we are willing to make to get there. We must understand that life comes with priorities. And we must be willing to let go of the idea that we can have it all. Making peace with these decisions will not be easy, but it will help silence the anxiety alarms.

Do you want to be a senior executive and make hundreds of thousands of dollars every year? Unless you work at an extraordinary company, you might need a nanny or a dedicated spouse to help you care for your kids. And you will probably miss ball games and dance recitals.

Do you want to stay at home and attend all your child's athletic performances and field trips? You might have to concede financially and be okay with making less money.

Can we all just stop and acknowledge the costs associated with the choices we make?

> " We must be willing to
>
> let go of the idea that
>
> we can have it all. "

While I have my own experiences and opinions, I'm not here to judge your life choices. As long as your decisions are intentional and made with wise counsel or with your spouse, your decisions are generally not good or bad. But *not* making decisions—keeping up with the grind and trying to have it all—is killing you.

You Have to Choose Your Ecosystem

I like to use the word *ecosystem* to help us think about the complexity of our lives and the world. Your ecosystem is the sum total of the world around you and the world within you—including your family history, where and how you grew up, the way you interact with your family and your community, the rules and expectations of your culture(s), your past traumas and joys, your physical health, and your thoughts, hopes, and actions. And for those of you who can't let this go—yes, even your genetics. Every part of your historical and current life makes up your ecosystem, like a group of a thousand tiny orchestra members coming together to play one beautiful symphony with the players and the songs constantly shuffling and changing.

So if your anxiety alarms are constantly sounding, chances are there are threats in your ecosystem. The sounding alarms mean your body has triggered your fight-or-flight-or-freeze response because something is very wrong, like: "Ahhh, a bear is coming!" or "Run! The neighboring city is attacking us!" or "Tom needs that spreadsheet PRONTO!" Our bodies often respond to the threats before we are consciously aware of them, beginning with elevated heart rates, intrusive thoughts, enlarged pupils, and a desire to go to war (fight), to run (flight), or to hide (freeze).

Most of us don't have bears chasing us anymore, but we do deal with small threats each day. We have to go to work and deal with that jerk Caleb in accounting. Or we have to see our old boyfriend Tucker every time we pass the mailroom at work. We're constantly slammed with negative images, dismissive attitudes, controlling in-laws, weather events, and political strife. We all carry around bricks of stress, neglect, and trauma in our backpacks that were put there by systems, past abuses, or tragic events. In this way, we encounter hundreds of small threats to our ecosystems every day. And these daily threats build on each other. Each day the alarms ring a bit louder and more often—and our backpacks keep getting heavier.

Just think about what now passes as a "normal" day: You're jolted awake by a clanging clock or a ringing cell phone (cue the stress hormones!). You load up on two or three cups of liquid stimulants (coffee or some spazzy energy drink) and rush around the house trying to get yourself, your kids, and the dog (that you didn't even want in the first place) ready for the day. After a chaotic merry-go-round, you jump in the car and smash the gas pedal down to the floor. You drive eighty miles per hour to work, weaving in and out of other metal death missiles (aka cars) on the highway. All the while, you're listening to the morning news of death, destruction, and division while scrolling social media (*why didn't Susan like my cat photo?*), trying to check your email, and rehearsing your first meeting of the day in your mind. You arrive at work, park in some soulless parking lot, and race up to your office, where you grab another coffee and a crummy pastry. And then you plop down in front of your computer where you'll spend most of the day, having your spirit sucked out of your body by a mixture of fluorescent lights, random deadlines, and TPS reports.

This is not a war zone or an uncommon experience. This is just any random Tuesday morning! Our ancient alarm systems that are supposed to remind us to stay with our tribe and avoid the lions don't stand a chance. If you throw in any type of deeper trauma or pain, such as physical or sexual abuse, neglect, abandonment, divorce, poverty, addiction, crime, or racism, your ecosystem remains devastated and constantly ringing the anxiety alarms.

To even further complicate matters, our ecosystems are changing faster than we can keep up. Psychologist Tal Ben-Shahar points out that "one of the reasons why depression and anxiety are on the rise throughout the world stems from the fast rate of change—markets change daily, technology advances by the nanosecond, and new ways of doing and being are constantly advertised and promoted."[7] The breakneck speed of change in our culture—the updates and notifications and trends and new releases and new cancellations—has us way over-stimulated and stressed out. We just weren't built for this endless stream of noise, demands, judgment, and fast-paced change.

> " The breakneck speed of change in our culture has us way overstimulated and stressed out. "

Most of us try to keep up with the rush of change until, suddenly, we run out of gas and just shut down. That's exactly what led a student of mine—we'll call him Mike—to visit me one day in my office. He was absolutely burned-out, exhausted, and empty. As he opened up about the paralyzing, around-the-clock anxiety he faced, I was able to act as a mirror to help him see that the anxiety wasn't to blame—his ecosystem was a mess. He was in his third year of law school, sleeping an average of four hours a night, living on energy drinks and Hot Pockets, and stressing out about taking the bar exam in a few months and landing the right job after graduation. On top of that, his dad couldn't stand him, his mom always called him to get his take on toxic news headlines, and his marriage was crumbling right in front of him. His wife had made huge sacrifices to help him through law school, but his physical, emotional, and spiritual absence from her during the past three years had frayed the threads of their marriage.

I helped Mike catch his breath and take an honest look at his ecosystem. *Of course he was stressed.* His anxiety alarms were ringing full blast because he didn't feel secure about his future or safe in his marriage. But really, his anxiety alarms were just doing their job. He was not healthy or heading in a direction toward wholeness. He was trying to do it all at the same time.

Thankfully, it ended well for Mike. He put down the things he could not control and bravely confronted the things he could control. He began seeing a counselor with his wife to heal his marriage. He prioritized sleep and eating right. He took walks and began writing down his thoughts to better identify where the anxiety was coming from. He challenged the catastrophic thoughts and quit reading all of the doomsday blogs and click-bait internet articles. He took comfort in the fact that he was in a difficult season—law school is super challenging (and it should be!)—and he had to submit to the necessary grind that studying, writing, and preparing would be. Mike quietly, and bravely, began the long road of honoring his wife and reconnecting with himself, he studied his butt off, and he passed the bar exam. Then, he followed his heart into public service where he is successfully serving those in his home community. Mike is a hero of mine, and we can learn from his story: you *can* make changes to your ecosystem and quiet the alarms.

Recognizing and acknowledging that your ecosystem is out of whack isn't easy, but doing just that can give you the perspective you need to reimagine a different future. Before you know it, you can begin connecting with others, changing your thoughts and your habits, and recognizing that hard seasons—and anxiety—do not have to last forever. Winter is uncomfortable, bleak, and gray . . . but spring is always on the way.

PART 2: HEALING FROM ANXIETY— FROM THE INSIDE OUT

All right, Delony . . . we get it! We're all anxious, burned-out, and exhausted. We're not medically or genetically programmed for a life of anxiety, medication isn't the only solution, anxiety isn't our identity or destiny, and we have some hard choices to make in order to change our ecosystems.

So what do you do now? Bottom line: you have to learn new skills, new ways of relating, thinking, and communicating, and then practice those new ways every day. But you *can* do this! And once you do, your shoulders will relax. You will sleep well on most nights. You will breathe instead of lashing out. You will roll your eyes at the intrusive thoughts you're having, and you will look people in the eye and connect with them while laughing from the bottom of your belly. Your default setting will be calm and joy first, anxiety and fear second (most of the time).

And before you know it, life will happen. Sure, you'll get a flat tire or a bad haircut, and a loved one will get sick. The stock market will crash and droughts and floods will come— but when you live a non-anxious life, you and your people will persevere, heal, serve others, and be at peace. You will lean on each other and make sure everyone is cared for and valued. You will sleep through the night. When the anxiety alarm sounds, you won't be terrified. Instead, you'll be notified.

One thing to remember: this is a Quick Read, but it's not a quick fix. So if you're not ready to take action, that's okay. Transformation isn't easy. Feel free to put this little book down and come back to it later. Give it to a friend or use it for two-ply on your next camping trip. Whatever works for you. But if you *are* ready to change your life, let's get going.

I've broken this next part into two sections: short-term actions and long-term changes. I want to give you some practical actions you can do right away when the alarms start clanging around in your heart and head, and I also want to provide you with long-term strategies for healing—because this is all about that long game.

Short-Term Actions You Can Start Today

1. Slow down and listen to the alarms.

Remember: anxiety is your body and your brain's way of trying to get your attention to let you know you are alone or not safe. When you feel your heart rate rising, or your palms sweating, or you wake up in the middle of the night once again, slow down, pause, and pay attention. What is your body telling you? What thoughts are running through your head? Ignoring the alarms, numbing them by mindlessly scrolling through Instagram, or trying to drown them out with that third beer or that thirteenth episode of your favorite show will only depress the problems and make them worse down the road. If you feel threatened, lonely, exhausted, or fixated on a person or situation that's causing you pain—it's time to slow down, listen, and get reacquainted with your ecosystem.

35

Practically speaking, here are a few habits you can develop
to pay better attention to what's going on in your head and in
your body:

**Write down the thoughts that are troubling you and
review for accuracy and truth.** Our feelings and intrusive thoughts are real and valid, but they don't always
tell the truth. That's why it's important to get your swirl-
ing blender of thoughts, criticisms, and failures out of
your head and down on paper. Once they're on paper,
you can go through them one by one and ask yourself
if they are true (it may help to do this with a trusted
friend, mentor, pastor, or counselor). Demand evidence
from your thoughts and behaviors. Are you really a terrible mom for forgetting lunchtime at school with your
daughter? Are you confident that you're the worst husband ever because you've gained thirty pounds over the
past few years? Is misplacing your car keys really an iron-
clad sign that you have pre-Alzheimer's disease?

> " Getting your thoughts out of
>
> your head and on to paper
>
> will help you determine what
>
> is true and what is not. "

Getting your thoughts out of your head and on to paper will help you determine what is true and what is not. Ultimately, this will help you learn the things you can control and things you can't control. Once you've practiced this over and over again, you'll begin to spot patterns in your thinking. This helps in two ways: You'll learn to quickly shut down the same, predictable lies that push you into a negative spiral. And you'll be able to identify sources of anxiety—and actually do something about it. This is a game changer when it comes to moving forward from your anxiety.

Be ready, though. Your thoughts and feelings may be telling you the truth. You may be in an unsafe relationship. Your credit card debt or student loans may have you close to ruin. You may need to move to a safer neighborhood. But now that you've separated fact from fiction, you can act and make changes.

Start a gratitude journal and begin to pray. I know—this might feel super lame. Do it anyway. The truth is, giving thanks forces you out of obsessing over the past (which you can't change) or the future (which you can't control), and brings your attention back to the present. Gratitude also helps turn your heart and mind from a mindset of scarcity and lack to one of blessing and enough. Practicing gratitude improves happiness, health, optimism, mood, sleep, and a sense of well-being.[8] Start or end every day by writing five different sentences that all begin with: "I'm grateful for . . . "

As far as prayer goes, I'm a Christian guy and my

belief in God informs how I live my life. Regular prayer is a deeply important practice to me. It's where I learn to give up control. Whether you're part of a formal faith group or not, you must submit yourself to the reality that there is something and someone out there bigger than you. If you don't know where to start with prayer, do a quick search for the full version of the Serenity Prayer—the classic prayer used in twelve-step programs all around the world. Even just the beginning of this prayer offers us some solid advice:

> *God, grant me the serenity*
> *to accept the things I cannot change;*
> *courage to change the things I can;*
> *and wisdom to know the difference.*[9]

Prayer reminds us that we are small and the world is gigantic. We can only control what is in our sphere—and we can let God handle the rest.

Find a person or group to be vulnerable with. Processing your thoughts and feelings out loud with a trusted friend, family member, counselor, or group can be transformative and healing. Connecting with a loved one—in person, face-to-face if possible—is one of the best ways to quickly calm your anxiety and regain a sense of safety. When connecting, you must commit to being courageous, vulnerable, and transparent. Brené Brown says it best: "Vulnerability sounds like truth and feels like courage. Truth and courage aren't always comfortable, but they're never weakness."[10] Courage and bravery and vulnerability help quiet our alarms.

> " The act of vulnerability and courage connects us to others by confirming a hidden universal truth: We are not alone. We all struggle. We all need each other. "

Full disclosure: I struggle with this. Being vulnerable and honest is hard for me. One of the chief demons of anxiety is that it makes you feel isolated and all alone. But the act of vulnerability and courage connects us to others by confirming a hidden universal truth: We are not alone. We all struggle. We all need each other.

Remember that an anxiety attack won't kill you (though it might feel like it). Anxiety doesn't execute you. It grinds you down. If you find yourself in a full-blown panic attack . . . breathe, drop your shoulders, and let it run its painful course. Don't fight it, kick it, or declare war on it. Just let it run. Learn to breathe deeply and steady your body. Call a doctor if you feel scared.

Over time, the more you choose *not* to fight things you can't control, the more your body will stop using panic and extreme flight to get your attention.

2. Learn to control your thoughts and actions.

Most of us don't challenge the thoughts that pop into our heads. We don't challenge where the thoughts came from, whose voice spoke them into being, or what hurt they're trying to protect us from. And most of us don't challenge our default actions, like yelling at someone when we're driving, snapping back at a social media comment, or threatening our kids over some nonsense. It's so important to keep in mind that our thoughts determine our actions and emotions. But—and stay with me on this—our actions and emotions then begin to determine our thoughts. They all reinforce each other and strengthen our behavior patterns. It's a dance between two unlikely partners—and you're caught in the middle.

> " You can't stop the thoughts that pop into your mind, but you can control what thoughts you give an audience to. "

What you have to remember is there's a clear starting point: your thoughts. If you want to change how you feel and act, start by working to control your thoughts. You can't stop the thoughts that pop into your mind, but you can control what thoughts you listen to, respond to, or give an audience to. Start to question your thoughts—especially the super dark ones or the super unrealistic ones. You must stop endlessly searching for data that backs up what you think, and you must stop being a victim of your own spiraling anxiety cycles. Ask yourself for evidence to support the thoughts that are setting off your alarms.

Here's an example of how easy it is to jump from a reasonable, healthy thought to an intrusive, worst-case scenario death spiral: Let's say you're on the dating scene and you see someone attractive at a party. You take a risk by walking across the room and striking up a conversation. After a few minutes of pleasant chatting, they excuse themselves to get a drink or to talk to another friend. They don't make an effort to see you again for the rest of the night. Of course, you're disappointed. You were courageous and vulnerable, and things didn't go the way you hoped.

You might think, *It sucks that [insert person's name] didn't want to hang out more.* This is a reasonable response. But within a split second, you jump from mild disappointment to something that feels more real: *But of course they don't want to hang out with me. I'm almost thirty, and I still get zits. And I'm super annoying . . . at least that's what my dad used to say. He's totally right. I'll never find anyone until I quit being so annoying. There's for sure something wrong with me. No one ever wants to hang out with me. It always ends up like this. I'll always be alone. I'll never have a family.*

That feels over the top when you read it, doesn't it? On paper, it looks silly. But in our heads, this can feel real—because our thoughts recruit our heart rates, our stress hormones, our clenched muscles, and our guts. When we're having a physical reaction to our anxious thoughts, it's hard to separate fact from fiction. Then, we spiral out of control and often talk to ourselves in ways we'd never let someone talk to a complete stranger. So don't talk to yourself that way! Be kind to yourself. Challenge the critical voice inside your head. Don't be a victim of your own thoughts or feelings.

> " Challenge the critical voice inside your head. Don't be a victim of your own thoughts or feelings. "

Let's dive a little deeper. If you've allowed your thoughts to rule you for most of your life, you're going to have to learn to take back control—and this is a process. It's just like learning to shoot a basketball or use a drill. It's a skill. You can start taking control of your thoughts by building these habits:

Get in touch with your thoughts through mindfulness. Mindfulness is the art and practice of being still while focusing on your breath and your body. It's all about being present with your thoughts, your body, and your environment. Through mindfulness, you'll learn how to have a new relationship with your thoughts and learn to take control of them so you can reset your default responses.

It's just like building a new muscle. That means learning to control your thoughts can feel challenging at first, but it gets easier as you get stronger over time. If you need a place to start, there are a number of meditation apps to help. I have been regularly meditating for over a decade, and it's been a true game changer for me.

Make a list of what you can and can't control. Anxiety often stems from a fear of the future and a lack of control. As I noted above, it is important to name what you can control, like your thoughts and actions, relationships, boundaries, work ethic, screen time, exercise plan, sleep, diet, how much debt you have, and how you respond to others. It's equally important to name the things you can't control. You can't control other people—their attitudes, insecurities, lack of boundaries, or behaviors. For example, you can't control what people post on social media, but you can delete the app from your phone. Control what you can and let everything else go.

Match your words with your pictures. We speak with words, but we think in pictures. Most of the time our pictures of how we *want* life to go don't line up with reality. If your marriage, your job, your children, your friends, your body, or your living situation don't look like you hoped they would by this point in your life, call it out. Own it. And make peace with the reality that is your current life.

We often create these pictures of our lives as children. Dr. Gabor Maté, an addiction and trauma physician and researcher, notes that "we create meanings from our unconscious interpretation of early events, and then we forge our present experiences from the meanings we've created. Unwittingly, we write the story of our future from narratives based on the past."[11]

It's time to turn the page on the stories of your past

and pick up your pen

to write something new.

Process your past hurts and trauma. I can't write about anxiety without addressing trauma. If you've experienced trauma (spoiler alert: most of us have), you must choose to reconcile your past to your present and create a plan for healing. Here's how you can start to process your hurt in three concrete steps:

Step 1: Acknowledge that the trauma (or hurt) exists. Simply naming your trauma is a powerful and healing process. If you ever want to move past your hurt, you must first identify it.

Step 2: Decide that you won't allow your trauma to become an identity. It's not enough to identify your hurt, slap a "survivor" sticker on your shirt pocket, and cling to unhealthy life and relationship patterns. Your past is an experience, not your destination. You are not the worst thing that ever happened to you.

You are not the worst thing you ever did. You are not the meanest thing you ever said that you wish you could take back. You must make up your mind to set the bricks of trauma down.

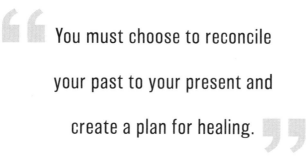

> **You must choose to reconcile your past to your present and create a plan for healing.**

Step 3: Work to run freely into your future and drop the trauma bricks of your past. You can do that by finding a therapist, a pastor, or a group of friends who will commit to walking you through this process for the long haul. You can choose to form new patterns of thinking and acting, but you cannot do it alone.

Let me illustrate this process with a story about a friend (we'll call him Drew) who sometimes experiences crippling social anxiety. As a kid, Drew's dad liked to point out to family friends how pudgy and nerdy Drew was. Drew's dad liked to make fun of his drawings, his straight A's, and how he couldn't get a date to prom. As a young adult, Drew was in a serious relationship with a girl he cared about. On the night he met her family for the first time, her father humiliated him by picking him apart in front of the entire family. For a number of reasons (the potential father-in-law being one of them), that relationship fizzled. He eventually fell in love with and married someone else.

Even though Drew's teenage years are behind him, and even though Drew's new in-laws are wonderful people, Drew has noticed that whenever he has dinner with his in-laws, he is overwhelmed by anxiety. The alarms start ringing because his brain and his body remember his past hurts and they are vigilant in reminding him: *Watch out! Don't get hurt again!* His chest tightens. His palms sweat. His heart rate rises. (Remember the fight-or-flight response?) He mumbles unfunny jokes that he regrets the moment he says them out loud. Sometimes, he can't even finish his food because he feels sick to his stomach—which is embarrassing for both him and his wife.

Thankfully, Drew had a lightbulb moment when he connected his current anxiety to his past trauma (Step 1: Acknowledgement). He also made up his mind that he doesn't want this to be his reality moving forward (Step 2: Rejecting trauma as an identity). Now, he's on to Step 3. He's talking about his challenges with a counselor and his wife—and he's taking active steps to own his thoughts and the reality of his present. By understanding how his alarms show up in his body and learning how to get in front of his thoughts before a night with the in-laws, he's able to actually enjoy those times, instead of dreading them. That's because Drew now understands where his feelings are coming from. He knows what's true and what's not true and that knowledge informs his actions.

Don't give your emotions the steering wheel. Feelings share valuable information with us about how we're interacting with the world, but they can't always be trusted. When you feel like a bad mom, a loser husband, a letdown employee, a bad friend, or a failure, it's important to acknowledge your feelings, write them down, and then check them for evidence. Feelings are often telling us different things than they originally let on. While you initially feel like the worst friend ever or a terrible husband—your feelings might just be letting you know that you need sleep, that you're disconnected and lonely, or that you need to have a very hard conversation at work. They might be reminding you to apologize, be more responsible, and change your priorities—or they might just be letting you know not to eat ice cream before bed.

Ultimately, feelings are signaling systems, not operating instructions. Imagine your feelings or emotions as traffic lights. Traffic signals don't tell us where to go or why we're going there. They don't dictate the music in the car, the conversations we have with our passengers, or how we will greet people at our destination. Traffic lights simply tell us when to stop or go, and we pay attention to them because we don't want to crash. But we don't let them tell us where we're headed. We need to stop letting the signals dictate our purposes, our boundaries, our needs, and our overall experiences.

Here's a recent example from my life. The other day I pulled into the parking lot at 8:30 a.m. As I was unloading my bag in my office, I got a call from my wife, asking me to check to see if her keys were in my car (apparently my son had accidently left *her* keys in *my* car when he was looking for a book—a classic ten-year-old boy move). *Oh, please no,* I thought to myself as I walked back to the parking lot. Sure enough, there they were, sitting on the back seat. Before I could blink, my heart rate spun up, and I got angry. My commute to work takes about thirty minutes. I looked at my watch: 8:33 a.m. My new show was set to begin recording at 9:30 a.m., meaning this hour-long round trip was going to cost me all of my prep time and probably make me late to the studio. There was little else I could do but jump in the car and race home.

My anger was a signal that things hadn't gone according to my plans, causing me to lose control of my precious schedule, which made *me* feel out of control. After thirty seconds of gripping the steering wheel tight enough to leave fingerprints in the leather, I smiled, let go, and remembered: *I get to decide how to respond.* Being angry or frustrated or driving like a maniac would not solve any of my problems, and it could only make them worse. Plus, my son is ten. He made a goof, like ten-year-olds do. After a few moments, I made up my mind not to be angry. Instead, I decided to take the rare unplanned hour in my day to listen to some music and prepare for my show in the car. I also decided to talk to my son about what happened only after I'd had some time to think about what I was going to say and how I could best teach him about responsibility. Showing up in a rage would only shut him down and make sure he wouldn't hear anything I said.

> " Let your emotions—anger, anxiety, sadness—inform you, but don't let them rule you. "

I'm no saint (this is my Quick Read, so I'm conveniently leaving out the times I've made bad decisions), but my decision to respond calmly and with control is something that we can all do. Let your emotions—anger, anxiety, sadness—inform you, but don't let them rule you. We get to decide how to control our thoughts and actions.

3. Breathe, eat, exercise, and sleep.

There's no easy way to say this: You have to take care of yourself if you want to silence the anxiety alarms. This is not a debate: we eat like trash, we don't move enough, and we don't get enough sleep. We are all capable of change, and we can all do better. I have to remind myself of that all the time (usually after eating a bag of marshmallows, drinking coffee at bedtime, and dominating some gummy candies). You can honor your heart, mind, and body by developing some simple routines:

Breathe. Remember the fight-or-flight response we talked about earlier? Deep breathing is one of the ways you can calm down your parasympathetic nervous system, which is the thing that triggers the fight-or-flight response. You can find tons of breathing exercises online. Personally, I use the box breathing method. This is how it works: inhale through your nose for four seconds, hold your breath for four seconds, and then exhale for four seconds. I repeat this for two to five minutes when I feel my alarms starting to wind up. I also do box breathing on long walks. It has a way of realigning everything.

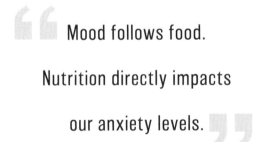

Mood follows food.

Nutrition directly impacts

our anxiety levels.

Eat nutritious food. Mood follows food. Nutrition directly impacts our anxiety levels. Most of us put our bodies into a heightened state of stress from the moment we wake up. Millions of us start our days by guzzling coffee, energy drinks, and eating refined carbs and sugar. Eating trash activates our alarm systems: too much caffeine spins up our heart rates, too much sugar and alcohol and carbs messes up our natural hormone responses, our sleep, and our brain's neurotransmitters.

And to top it all off, processed foods with all their artificial preservatives, colors, and additives are barely more nutritious than the cheapest dog food. You deserve better. We all must do better.

Exercise. Remember that anxiety is your body and your brain's way of preparing you for *action*. We get scared, our body floods itself with a ton of hormones, our pupils dilate, our shoulders tense up, our brains lock in, our hearts race, and our muscles tighten . . . and then we plop down on the couch and binge a show or look at our phones. When we don't move, our body has no way to process the flood of response chemicals that overwhelms us when the anxiety alarms are triggered.

Resist the urge to plop down in front of a screen. Put on your walking shoes and head outside, toss the ball with your kid, or start a push-up challenge with a friend. Then work on getting into a long-term exercise routine doing something you enjoy, whether it's running, hiking, or trying out a hip-hop dance class. Regular movement has literally hundreds of health benefits—one of them being a release of chemicals (like endorphins) in the brain that promote a sense of well-being.[12]

Sleep. As our society has gotten more hectic and rushed, we've sacrificed sleep in the name of productivity and accomplishment. Over the past sixty years, we've unceremoniously lopped off more than 25 percent of the sleep that our bodies need.[13] And it's killing us. A sleep-deprived brain is an anxious one—and a disturbed one. Neurologists and sleep researchers are uncovering shocking links between chronic lack of sleep and a host of health problems, including depression and anxiety. One study found that after a night of being subjected to no sleep, brain scans of participants showed decreased activation of the medial prefrontal cortex (that's the decision-making part of the brain that normally helps keep our anxiety in check). Additionally, the study found that while the thinking part of the brain slowed down, the brain's deeper emotional centers were overactive. Sleep researcher Dr. Matthew Walker explained, "Without sleep, it's almost as if the brain is too heavy on the emotional accelerator pedal, without enough brake."[14]

> " A sleep-deprived brain
>
> is an anxious one—and
>
> a disturbed one. "

Another study tracked sleep and saw anxiety levels change over four consecutive days. A lack of sleep or poor sleep quality was a reliable indicator that the participant would feel more anxious the next day. And on the flip side, those who got sufficient deep sleep had better moods and less anxiety. Dr. Walker sums it up best: "The best bridge between despair and hope is a good night of sleep."[15]

Long-Term Changes for Healing

Transforming your relationship with anxiety isn't an easy or short road, and you have to commit to these changes for the long haul. You'll need to constantly challenge your own thoughts and actions, check in with your community, and rethink the expectations you've created for your work, your relationships, and your legacy. This is a life-long commitment.

So in addition to the short-term strategies, I want to offer you deeper, long-term ways of reimagining and changing your life that will help you navigate your relationship with anxiety and restore health and peace.

1. Examine the ecosystem of your life.

If one (or many) aspects of your ecosystem are unhealthy, your entire ecosystem will be out of balance. To truly thrive and live a joyful, purposeful life, you must do the hard work of examining all aspects of who you are and what makes up your ecosystem. Remember that your ecosystem includes:

▾ Your physical, spiritual, and mental health
▾ Your relationships
▾ Your financial security
▾ Your cultural and family expectations
▾ Your current and past traumas
▾ Your living situation

- ▼ Your connection to meaningful work
- ▼ Your ability to feel safe, valued, and loved
- ▼ Your boundaries

Be aware that evaluating your ecosystem can be discouraging and even shame-inducing. If you've never done it before, I strongly recommend that you do it with a trusted friend, mentor, minister, or a therapist. Facing your reality can be a dark and lonely process. But if you desire peace and wholeness, you *must* take stock of where you are now so you can paint a picture of who and where you want to be. Below are some questions to help you begin to take stock of your life. I encourage you to write down your answers to these questions.

- ▼ How does my current environment make me feel safe? How does it make me feel valued?
- ▼ What past traumas and painful relationships have I not dealt with and need to address?
- ▼ Where are the spaces that I feel connected and am able to be vulnerable with others?
- ▼ In what ways is my work purposeful and meaningful, if at all?
- ▼ Am I honoring my body with good habits?
- ▼ How am I prioritizing my health (examples: eating well, exercising, and getting seven to nine hours of sleep every night)?
- ▼ What forms of distraction, numbing, or comfort am I addicted to?
- ▼ What feelings or fears make me retreat and hide or run to addiction?

These questions can be hard. You might work through them and realize that it's time to make big changes. Maybe it's time to end an intimate relationship or to find a new job. Maybe it's time to see a doctor or a counselor and regain control of your health. Maybe you need to cut cable and ditch social media. You don't have to fix everything right now—just take the next step and surround yourself with people you trust who can help you sort through these questions.

2. Learn how to grieve.

At first glance, the relationship between anxiety and grief might not seem obvious. But grief and anxiety are intimately connected. Grief provides an opportunity to examine the people and situations that have hurt us so we can learn from them and move forward. Grieving is about acknowledging, processing, and putting down the bricks of deep pain or regret, unmet expectations, shame, different life paths, or change. Unresolved grief can become a breeding ground for the nameless, low-level anxiety we can't shake.

Sadly, grieving is not something most of us do anymore. We are not taught how to grieve, and we don't talk about the cultural or spiritual importance of properly acknowledging and honoring losses or transitions. We're allowed to laugh, to be angry or mad, and to be happy (real or fake). But most of us don't have cultural space to be silent, to mourn, or to take time to process hard seasons or past hurts. Instead, we have quick fixes and immediate solutions. We have discipline and slogans. We have industries that thrive off of helping us hide our discomfort—as if happiness is just a swipe away.

Because of that, we often don't acknowledge what we've lost

or what didn't happen (even though we hoped and longed for it). These wounds stay open so we can't transition and heal. And I'm not just talking about the big things, like the death of a loved one or being unable to conceive a child. Grief hits us in the small ways too. Like having to cancel your summer vacation because of the 2020 pandemic, or suddenly being thrust into homeschooling, or having to quit your job to care for your aging parents, or spraining your ankle the day before the big race. Unexpected loss and change come at all of us, all of the time. We must take time to acknowledge the grief in order to properly transition to what's next.

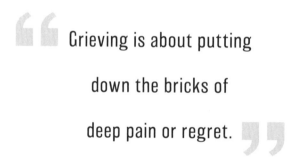

Grieving is about putting down the bricks of deep pain or regret.

When you are grieving, resist the temptation to compare your losses to the losses of others. Comparing grief sets us up for an endless cycle of minimizing our pain or judging everyone else. I've seen this during the COVID-19 pandemic. It goes something like this: *Yeah, we had to cancel my son's birthday party, but one of my friends had to postpone her wedding. Yeah, I had to postpone my wedding, but at least I still have my job. Well, I lost my job, but at least no one in my family has died.* This approach is problematic for two reasons: it limits your ability to grieve, and though it might seem noble, minimizing or judging grief doesn't actually accomplish anything. You're not helping other people feel better by denying your own loss and pain. Hiding your hurt doesn't make it go away. Own your grief and don't apologize for it. And let other people have theirs.

Acknowledging what you've lost shines a light on your pain. Light takes away the power and mystery of darkness. We will never heal from our trauma until we've processed it. We will never move on until we've allowed ourselves to feel the weight of the loss and hurt so we can make sense of it all. Give yourself permission to grieve. Cry. Yell. Be angry. Connect with a trusted friend or a therapist to work through lingering pain. Sit in your pain and loss, maybe even schedule time with it, but don't bathe in it. Eventually, you will move through the grief and find meaning on the other side. Acknowledging loss and finding meaning helps us silence the alarms.

3. See a professional therapist.

A good therapist can help you change the way you talk to yourself and how you interact with others. A good counselor can help you become self-aware and recognize when you're living in fantasy land, indulging in distorted patterns of thinking, or telling yourself false stories. A good therapist helps you process trauma, learn new skills for acting and thinking, and practice new ways of being. Therapy isn't about getting rid of all the problems in your life. It's about learning that you have the ability to face those problems and grow through them. Only rarely have I met someone who thought therapy was a waste of time. Even then, it was usually because that person had connected with a poor therapist, or the person wasn't ready to be honest and vulnerable. A good therapist is worth their weight in gold.

Throughout my life, I have met with a counselor, a psychologist, a marriage and family therapist, ministers, coaches, and several mentors. I have relationships with traditional doctors and a holistic doctor. All of them are skilled and excellent in their own ways. I cannot express how important and helpful professional, qualified mental health or relational help can be. I strongly recommend meeting with a mental health professional or another trained, neutral third party, as often as you need or are able to. Remember: you don't have to be in crisis mode to make an appointment.

4. Invest in new or existing relationships.

This is perhaps the most important truth you will read in this entire Quick Read: you need other people. Connection heals anxiety.

We're disconnected and fragmented. Our spouses don't really know us, our friends don't really know us, our pretend internet communities definitely don't know us, and often, we don't even know ourselves. That's why loneliness is the chief enemy of our modern world. When we're lonely, we make up stories about why we're hurting. We tell ourselves stories of abandonment and unworthiness and shame. We make enemies out of our neighbors, turning "us" into "them." The toll of loneliness on our bodies—the actual biochemical poison that our brain creates when it recognizes that it is lonely—is worse for us than smoking cigarettes.[16] Loneliness is killing us.

Think of relationships as the emergency fund for our lives; they rescue us with a soft place to land. When trouble strikes, people keep us grounded when we encounter stress and difficulty. They provide security, wisdom, and even a warm meal.

> **You need other people.**
>
> **Connection heals anxiety.**

You can find that kind of connection by joining a community, allowing yourself to be vulnerable with those you trust, and making sure to connect in person. It doesn't have to be hard—just invite people into your existing routines. Investing in deep relationships will help heal you—your life will improve when your relationships do.

CONCLUSION

Every once in a while, I think about the day I got in my wife's little Corolla, drove to a different town, and walked into my friend's office to ask for help. I remember being vulnerable for the first time about my anxiety, acknowledging that I needed help changing jobs, imagining a new future, and working to repair or end failing relationships. I remember learning new skills—like how to create boundaries and say no—and realizing that I wasn't the center of the universe. I am still on this journey.

Fast-forward to now. I live in a different state and have two children who are growing up fast. I no longer work at a university, and I don't make many late-night hospital visits. My marriage is better than it has ever been and, thankfully, I'm continually becoming a different man than I once was.

On most days, I choose to wake up with a smile. I see and feel the weight of a mad, violent, and chaotic world, and usually, I make the choice to separate the things I can control from the things that I cannot. To do that, I have a daily gratitude practice and a morning routine I honor on most days. I submit to mentors and my church leaders and work outside with my hands as often as possible. I'm militant about getting eight hours of sleep and daily exercise—but I don't beat myself up if I wake up at 2:00 a.m. or skip a workout. I keep social media on a separate device, and I only use it for work. (I make myself look at eyes, not screens.) I haven't taken anxiety medication in years, and I keep a rotation of supplements and dietary practices that I've found work to keep me healthy and whole.

I still feel deeply and have a tendency toward being either overly cautious and anxious or carefree and reckless. But I've worked hard to examine my ecosystem, to learn to listen and understand my alarms, and to change the things that I can. Some of these changes took days. Others took years. And some of my tendencies will be with me forever, like my need for touch, my tendency to isolate, my love for old heavy metal CDs and Will Ferrell and Adam Sandler movies.

I'm not special or unique in any way. I am like you. And like you, I was sick and tired of being sick and tired. I was exhausted by the fatigue and tired of the deafening alarms. I was tired of hurting others and of always being hurt. I had enough of letting anxiety run my life. So I took back control by letting a lot of things go. And if I can do it, you can too.

We are in this together. There are countless numbers of people who have said, "No More!" to the myths about anxiety and to living life in a defensive, anxious position.

I want to encourage you to cry the tears, feel the sweat, and acknowledge the feelings of powerlessness and despair. If someone you love struggles with anxiety, I want you to know that their feelings can be dark, never-ending, and relentless. But I also want you to know that you and your loved ones can become whole and well and free from those shrieking anxiety alarms and out-of-control bodies. You can decide to work on yourself, your relationships, and your ecosystem.

> " You are worth being well and
> you are worth a full night of sleep.
> You are worth being loved and
> loving others. And you are
> most certainly not alone. "

You are worth being well and you are worth a full night of sleep. You are worth being loved and loving others. And you are most certainly not alone. There are many of us wandering these old roads to freedom. Anxiety has lost its grip on our throats, and we're there for each other on the rare days it pops back up.

There is healing, hope, and wellness for you on the other side of anxiety. You *can* take the next step and move forward! Start now.

NOTES

1. "Facts and Statistics," Anxiety and Depression Association of America, accessed September 23, 2020, https://adaa.org/about-adaa/press-room/facts-statistics.

2. Substance Abuse and Mental Health Services Administration, *Impact of the DSM-IV to DSM-5 Changes on the National Survey on Drug Use and Health [Internet]*, (Rockville, MD: Substance Abuse and Mental Health Services Administration (US), June 2016), https://www.ncbi.nlm.nih.gov/books/NBK519704/table/ch3.t15/, table 3.15, "DSM-IV to DSM-5 Generalized Anxiety Disorder Comparison."

3. Brené Brown, *Rising Strong: How the Ability to Reset Transforms the Way We Live, Love, Parent, and Lead* (New York: Random House, 2015), 241.

4. Kristen L. Syme and Edward H. Hagen, "Mental Health Is Biological Health: Why Tackling 'Diseases of the Mind' Is an Imperative for Biological Anthropology in the 21st Century," *Yearbook of Physical Anthropology* 171, suppl. 70 (October 24, 2019), 93, https://doi.org/10.1002/ajpa.23965.

5. Anthony F. Jorm, Scott B. Patten, Traolach S. Brugha, and Ramin Mojtabai, "Has Increased Provision of Treatment Reduced the Prevalence of Common Mental Disorders? Review of the Evidence from Four Countries," *World Psychiatry* 16, no. 1 (February 2017), 90–99, https://doi.org/10.1002/wps.20388.

6. "Anxiety Statistics, Facts Information," Anxietycentre.com, last updated July 1, 2020, https://www.anxietycentre.com/anxiety-statistics-information.shtml.

7. Tal Ben-Shahar, *The Pursuit of Perfect: How to Stop Chasing Perfection and Start Living a Richer, Happier Life* (UK: McGraw-Hill Education, 2009), 26–27.

8. Kori D. Miller, "14 Health Benefits of Practicing Gratitude According to Science," PositivePsychology.com, January 9, 2020, https://positivepsychology.com/benefits-of-gratitude/.

9. Chad Napier, "What Is the Serenity Prayer? Is it Biblical?" Christianity.com, May 5, 2020, https://www.christianity.com /wiki/prayer/what-is-the-serenity-prayer-is-it-biblical.html.

10. Brené Brown, *Daring Greatly* (New York: Avery, 2012), 37.

11. Gabor Maté, MD, *In the Realm of Hungry Ghosts: Close Encounters with Addiction* (Berkeley, CA: North Atlantic Books, 2010), 370.

12. Elizabeth Anderson and Geetha Shivakumar, "Effects of Exercise and Physical Activity on Anxiety," *Frontiers in Psychiatry 4, no. 23 (April 2013),* https://doi.org/10.3389/fpsyt.2013.00027.

13. Matthew Walker, PhD, *Why We Sleep, Unlocking the Power of Sleep and Dreams,* (Scribner, 2017).

14. Eti Ben Simon, Aubrey Rossi, Allison G. Harvey, and Matthew P. Walker, "Overanxious and Underslept," *Nature Human Behavior* 4 (January 2020), 100–110, https://doi.org/10.1038 /s41562-019-0754-8.

15. Ben Simon et al., "Overanxious and Underslept," 100–110.

16. Nick Tate, "Loneliness Rivals Obesity, Smoking as Health Risk," WebMD, May 4, 2018, https://www.webmd.com/balance/news /20180504/loneliness-rivals-obesity-smoking-as-health-risk.

ABOUT THE AUTHOR

Dr. John Delony is a leading voice on relationships and mental health. Prior to joining Ramsey Solutions, John worked in crisis response and as a senior leader at multiple universities. He holds two PhDs—one in counseling and one in higher education. Now as the host of *The Dr. John Delony Show*, John guides callers through real-life relationship and mental health challenges. For more information, visit johndelony.com.

Answering Life's Messy Questions

The Dr. John Delony Show is a caller-driven show that helps you find the answers to questions about mental health, wellness, relationships, and more.

www.johndelony.com